MATHS TODAY

for ages 9 - 10

Addition

Subtraction

Multiplication

Division

Negative Numbers

Money

Length

Perimeter

Time

Lines and Shapes

Symmetry

Handling Data

Pictograms

Number Lines

Number Problems

Complete these additions as quickly as you can:

ⓐ	ⓑ	ⓒ	ⓓ	ⓔ	ⓕ
236 + 152	418 + 237	365 + 365	548 + 193	306 + 299	611 + 289

Minnie

Sometimes we need to add together more than two numbers.

If we want to add together these numbers:

36, 457 and 8

... we must write them out in the correct columns:

Max

It's easy, if you remember to write the units in line.

The numbers are written in the correct columns.

Look how carefully the units are lined up.

```
H T U
  3 6
4 5 7
+   8
_____
```

Add the units first:

6 + 7 + 8 = 21

We write 1 in the units answer and 2 under the tens.

```
  3 6
4 5 7
+   8
_____
    1
  2
```

Now add the tens:

3 + 5 + 2 = 10

We write 0 in the tens answer and 1 under the hundreds.

```
  3 6
4 5 7
+   8
_____
  0 1
1 2
```

Add the hundreds:

4 + 1 = 5

So the final answer is   501

```
  3 6
4 5 7
+   8
_____
5 0 1
1 2
```

Complete these additions.
The numbers have already been put into the correct columns for you:

ⓖ	ⓗ	ⓘ	ⓙ	ⓚ	ⓛ
329 46 + 118	208 427 + 36	598 3 + 27	45 76 + 204	333 264 + 159	250 175 + 175

Some people prefer to write the biggest number at the top ...

... and the smallest number at the bottom.

If we need to add these numbers ...

27, 594 and 217

... we can write them in the correct columns like this:

```
  5 9 4
  2 1 7
+   2 7
───────

───────
```

Complete these additions, writing the numbers in order of size. Remember how important it is to put the figures in the correct columns. The first one has been written out for you.

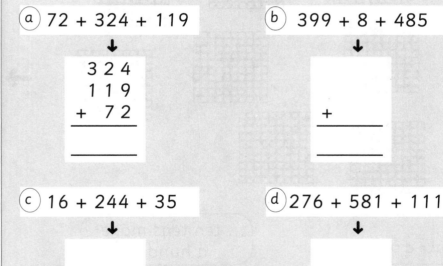

a) 72 + 324 + 119

```
  3 2 4
  1 1 9
+   7 2
───────

───────
```

b) 399 + 8 + 485

```
+
───

───
```

c) 16 + 244 + 35

```
+
───

───
```

d) 276 + 581 + 111

```
+
───

───
```

e) 5 + 89 + 642

```
+
───

───
```

f) 409 + 32 + 284

```
+
───

───
```

Thousands, Hundreds, Tens and Units

□ ← *If we say that this little square is a unit, we can join ten of them together …*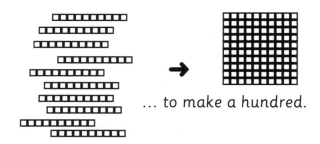

… *to make a ten.*

We can join ten tens together …

… *to make a hundred.*

We can join ten hundreds together to make a thousand.

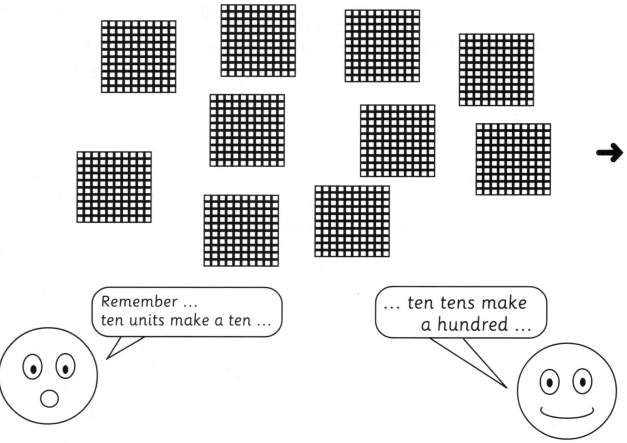

*Remember …
ten units make a ten …*

*… ten tens make
a hundred …*

… and ten hundreds make a thousand.

1 x 10 = 10   10 x 100 = 1000

10 x 10 = 100

10 x 1 = 10   100 x 10 = 1000

Adding with thousands, hundreds, tens and units is easy.

Don't forget to write neatly and to put the numbers in the correct columns.

```
Th H T U
 2 6 4 8
+    7 9 4
_____
```

Add the units first, then the tens, then the hundreds, then the thousands.

```
Th H T U
 2 6 4 8
+    7 9 4
_____
 3 4 4 2
  1 1 1
```

Complete these additions as quickly as you can:

a)
```
  3976
+ 1419
_____
```

b)
```
  6432
+ 2698
_____
```

c)
```
  8117
+  699
_____
```

d)
```
  5480
+ 3679
_____
```

e)
```
  4999
+    1
_____
```

f) 2104 + 516 + 1937
↓

```
+
___
___
```

g) 619 + 3742 + 2898
↓

```
+
___
___
```

A thousand

Try to answer these questions:

h) What number is half of ten? ☐

i) What number is half of a hundred? ☐

j) What number is half of a thousand? ☐

5

Subtraction

When you have to find the difference between two numbers you can use subtraction.

Remember to always write the bigger number at the top.

For example, to find the difference between 32 and 497 we would write the question out like this:

$$\begin{array}{r} 497 \\ -\ 32 \\ \hline \end{array}$$

↖ Because 497 is bigger than 32 it goes at the top.

Use subtraction to answer the questions below.
Remember to write the bigger number at the top.
The first one has been written out for you.

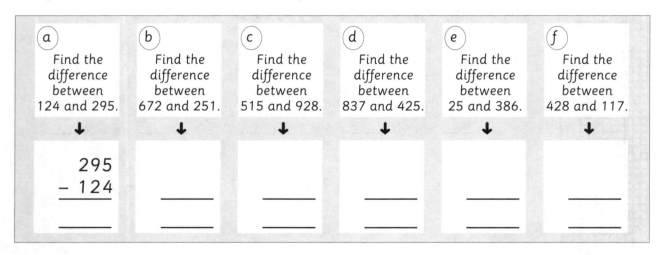

a	b	c	d	e	f
Find the difference between 124 and 295.	Find the difference between 672 and 251.	Find the difference between 515 and 928.	Find the difference between 837 and 425.	Find the difference between 25 and 386.	Find the difference between 428 and 117.
↓	↓	↓	↓	↓	↓

$$\begin{array}{r} 295 \\ -\ 124 \\ \hline \end{array}$$

In this question there are not enough units at the top ...

... so we can make ten extra units by using one of the tens.

$$\begin{array}{r} 673 \\ -355 \\ \hline \end{array}$$

↘

$$\begin{array}{r} 6\ \overset{6}{\cancel{7}}{}^{1}3 \\ -355 \\ \hline \end{array}$$

In the top number there are now 6 tens instead of 7 and there are 13 units.

Complete the subtractions below.
Make some extra units from a ten if you need to.

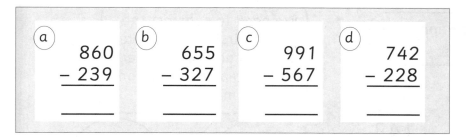

(a)	(b)	(c)	(d)
860	655	991	742
− 239	− 327	− 567	− 228
———	———	———	———

Sometimes there are not enough tens so we make extra tens by using one of the hundreds..

$$627$$
$$-153$$
———

➤

$$\overset{5}{6}\,{}^{1}2\,7$$
$$-1\;5\;3$$
———

In the top number there are now 5 hundreds instead of 6 and there are 12 tens.

Complete the subtractions below.
ALWAYS START WITH THE UNITS.
If there are not enough units, make some from a ten.
If there are not enough tens, make some from a hundred.
Remember that if you already have enough, you don't need to make extra units or extra tens.

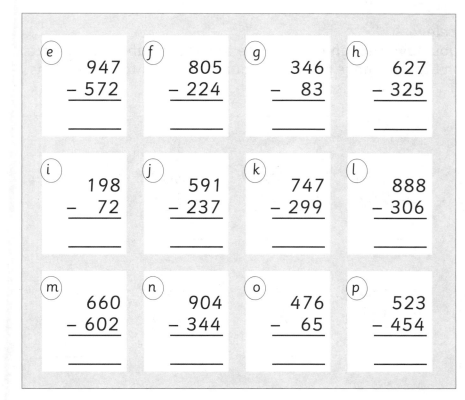

(e)	(f)	(g)	(h)
947	805	346	627
− 572	− 224	− 83	− 325
———	———	———	———

(i)	(j)	(k)	(l)
198	591	747	888
− 72	− 237	− 299	− 306
———	———	———	———

(m)	(n)	(o)	(p)
660	904	476	523
− 602	− 344	− 65	− 454
———	———	———	———

Number Speed

Digital Stopwatch
Mins : Secs
00:00

How quickly can you answer these questions?
Time yourself and record your score.

1) $8 - 4 =$

2) $18 - 4 =$

3) $28 - 4 =$

4) $38 - 4 =$

5) $78 - 4 =$

6) $9 - 3 =$

7) $29 - 3 =$

8) $99 - 3 =$

9) $12 - 7 =$

10) $22 - 7 =$

11) $52 - 7 =$

12) $14 - 8 =$

13) $24 - 8 =$

14) $34 - 8 =$

15) $84 - 8 =$

16) $11 - 6 =$

17) $21 - 6 =$

18) $61 - 6 =$

19) $13 - 5 =$

20) $43 - 5 =$

Time taken:

☐ minutes and

☐ seconds.

Look what happens in this question.

We need to subtract the 8 units first, but there are no units on the top line and no tens to make some units from.

$$
\begin{array}{r}
700 \\
- 148 \\
\hline
\end{array}
$$

Step One

We will make ten tens by using one of the hundreds.

Cross out the 7 in the hundreds column and write a 6. Then put a little 1 to show that we have ten tens.

$$
\begin{array}{r}
^6 \cancel{7} 0\,0 \\
- 1\,4\,8 \\
\hline
\end{array}
$$

Step Two

We will make ten units by using one of the ten tens.

Cross out the 10 in the tens column and write a 9. Then put a little 1 to show that we have ten units.

$$
\begin{array}{r}
^6 \cancel{7} \, ^9\cancel{0}\, 0 \\
- 1\,4\,8 \\
\hline
\end{array}
$$

Step Three

Now the subtraction is easy:

10 units subtract 8 makes 2.

9 tens subtract 4 makes five.

6 hundreds subtract 1 makes 5.

$$
\begin{array}{r}
^6 \cancel{7} \, ^9\cancel{0}\, ^1 0 \\
- 1\,4\,8 \\
\hline
5\,5\,2
\end{array}
$$

Complete the subtractions below.
ALWAYS start by seeing if you have enough units on the top line to subtract the units on the bottom line. You don't always have to make ten units out of a ten or ten tens out of a hundred.

a)
$$
\begin{array}{r}
700 \\
- 239 \\
\hline
\end{array}
$$

b)
$$
\begin{array}{r}
600 \\
- 499 \\
\hline
\end{array}
$$

c)
$$
\begin{array}{r}
984 \\
- 263 \\
\hline
\end{array}
$$

d)
$$
\begin{array}{r}
500 \\
- 68 \\
\hline
\end{array}
$$

e)
$$
\begin{array}{r}
803 \\
- 276 \\
\hline
\end{array}
$$

f)
$$
\begin{array}{r}
719 \\
- 527 \\
\hline
\end{array}
$$

g)
$$
\begin{array}{r}
432 \\
- 268 \\
\hline
\end{array}
$$

h)
$$
\begin{array}{r}
200 \\
- 39 \\
\hline
\end{array}
$$

i)
$$
\begin{array}{r}
598 \\
- 119 \\
\hline
\end{array}
$$

j)
$$
\begin{array}{r}
703 \\
- 247 \\
\hline
\end{array}
$$

k)
$$
\begin{array}{r}
981 \\
- 536 \\
\hline
\end{array}
$$

l)
$$
\begin{array}{r}
684 \\
- 354 \\
\hline
\end{array}
$$

Now try some subtractions with thousands, as well as hundreds, tens and units.

Remember how important it is to write the numbers in the correct columns.

If you haven't got enough hundreds you can make ten hundreds by using one of the thousands, just like you can make ten units by using a ten or ten tens by using a hundred.

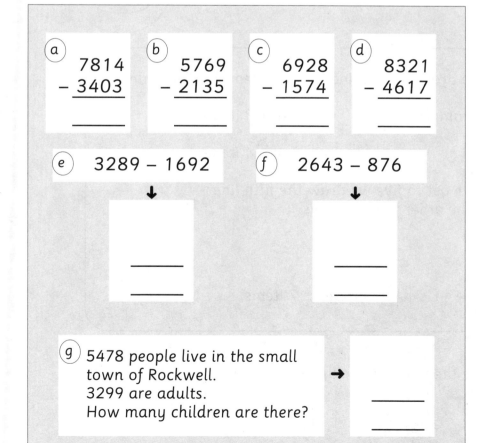

a)
```
  7814
- 3403
------
```

b)
```
  5769
- 2135
------
```

c)
```
  6928
- 1574
------
```

d)
```
  8321
- 4617
------
```

e) 3289 – 1692

f) 2643 – 876

g) 5478 people live in the small town of Rockwell. 3299 are adults. How many children are there?

Number Speed

Digital Stopwatch
Mins : Secs
00:00

Find the missing numbers in the questions below.

1)   + 7 = 10

2)   6 +   = 9

3)   + 4 = 11

4)   + 8 = 15

5)   9 +   = 17

6)   12 +   = 19

7)   + 7 = 19

8)   8 +   = 12

9)   13 +   = 18

10) 14 +   = 20

11) 12 –   = 8

12) 13 –   = 8

13) 14 –   = 8

14) 15 –   = 8

15) 16 –   = 8

16) 17 –   = 8

17)   – 6 = 12

18)   – 7 = 12

19)   – 4 = 9

20)   – 5 = 8

Time taken:

☐ minutes and

☐ seconds.

Handling Data

Count the number of squares, circles and triangles shown here:

(i) How many squares do you think there are?

(ii) How many circles do you think there are?

(iii) How many triangles do you think there are?

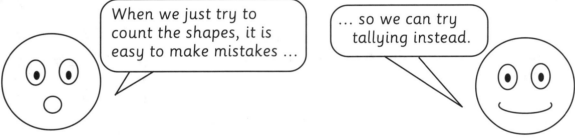

When we just try to count the shapes, it is easy to make mistakes ...

... so we can try tallying instead.

When we tally, we draw a short line for each item that we count:

    ... so, for example, | | | represents 3 items,

                             | | | | represents 4 items.

When we get to five we draw the fifth line across the other four, like this: ЖТ

ЖТ | | represents 7 items.

What numbers do the following tally marks show?

(a) ЖТ |

(b) ЖТ | | |

(c) ЖТ ЖТ

(d) ЖТ ЖТ |

(e) | | |

(f) ЖТ ЖТ ЖТ

Now we will use tallying to find the number of squares, circles and triangles.

The squares have been done for you.

Each square has been crossed out and a tally mark has been made for each one.

Now do the same for the circles and triangles. When you have finished tallying you will be able to write in the number of each shape.

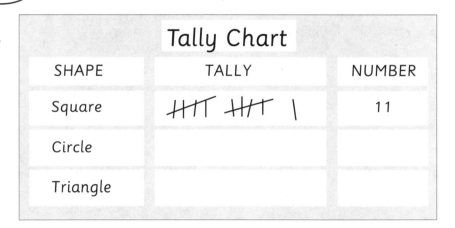

Tally Chart

SHAPE	TALLY	NUMBER
Square	H̶I̶T̶ H̶I̶T̶ \	11
Circle		
Triangle		

Now find the number of boats and aeroplanes by tallying.
Remember to cross each one out as you tally it so that you don't lose count.

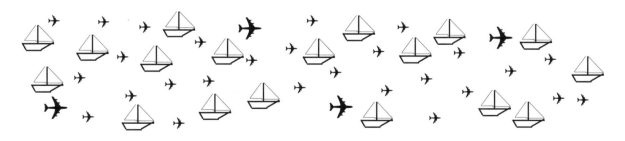

OBJECT	TALLY	NUMBER
Aeroplane		
Boat		

Here is a short passage from a story:

David wheeled his new bike out of the garage.
He was particularly pleased with the metal
parts, which were bronze coloured instead of
the usual chrome or aluminium.

Use the tallying method to find the number of times that each letter of the alphabet appears in the passage.

Remember to cross out each letter as you tally. Some letters have been done for you.

Tally Chart

	TALLY	NUMBER		TALLY	NUMBER
a	⊬⊬ ⊬⊬ ‖	12	n		
b	|	2	o		
c	|||	4	p		
d	⊬⊬ |	6	q		
e			r		
f			s		
g			t		
h			u		
i			v		
j			w		
k			x		
l			y		
m			z		

Now transfer your data onto a bar chart.
The first four letters have been done for you.

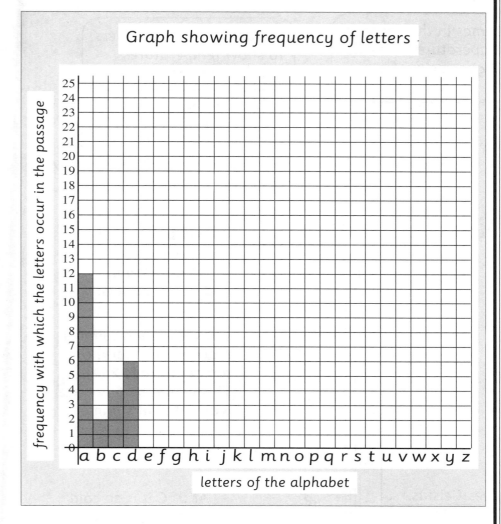

Graph showing frequency of letters

frequency with which the letters occur in the passage

letters of the alphabet

These letters are called vowels:

a e i o u

All the other letters are called consonants.

Use the bar chart to help you to answer the following questions about the letters found in the passage.

(a) Which is the most common vowel in the passage about David's bike?

(b) Which is the most common consonant in the passage about David's bike?

(c) Which letters appear less than three times?

(d) Which letters appear ten times or more?

Number Speed

Digital
Stopwatch
Mins : Secs
00:00

Fill in the missing digit for each question below.

1) 4☐ + 7 = 50

2) 23 + ☐7 = 50

3) 3 + 4☐ = 50

4) 26 + ☐4 = 40

5) ☐6 + 24 = 40

6) ☐6 + 4 = 40

7) ☐2 + 18 = 30

8) 2☐ + 2 = 30

9) 8 + ☐☐ = 30

10) 3☐ + 22 = 60

11) ☐8 + 32 = 60

12) 42 + 1☐ = 60

13) ☐8 + 12 = 60

14) 29 + 4☐ = 70

15) 31 + ☐9 = 70

16) 19 + ☐1 = 70

17) 36 + 4☐ = 80

18) 2☐ + 53 = 80

19) 49 + ☐1 = 80

20) 6☐ + 12 = 80

Time taken:

☐ minutes and

☐ seconds.

Negative Numbers

Sometimes in the winter the temperature is so cold that it goes below freezing point.

We use negative numbers to show temperatures which are below freezing.

Look carefully at this picture of a thermometer:

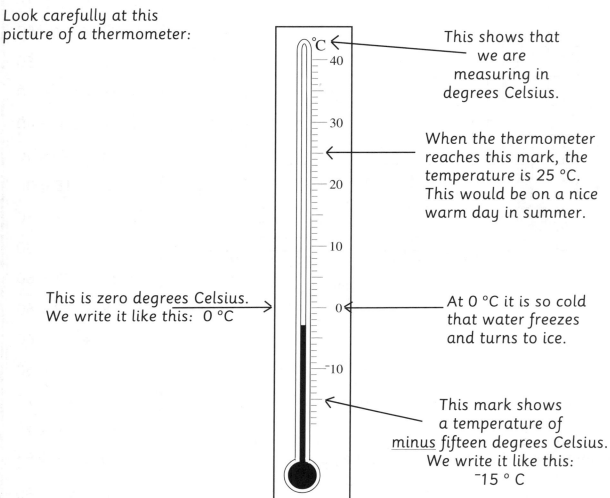

This shows that we are measuring in degrees Celsius.

When the thermometer reaches this mark, the temperature is 25 °C. This would be on a nice warm day in summer.

This is zero degrees Celsius. We write it like this: 0 °C

At 0 °C it is so cold that water freezes and turns to ice.

This mark shows a temperature of minus fifteen degrees Celsius. We write it like this: ¯15 ° C

This thermometer currently shows a temperature of ¯3 °C. This would be on a cold day in winter.

a) What is the highest temperature which can possibly be shown on this thermometer?

b) What is the lowest temperature which can possibly be shown on this thermometer?

The temperature shown on the thermometer on page 14 is minus three degrees Celsius.

We write this temperature like this: $^-3\ °C$

Notice the little minus sign in front of the number 3.

Write down the temperature which is shown on each of the thermometers below:

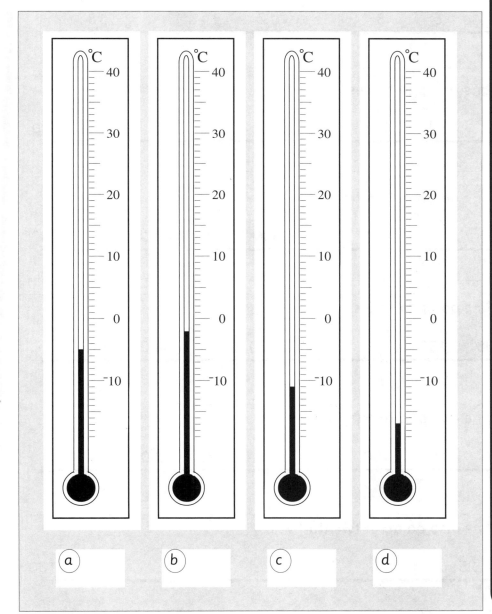

Digital
Stopwatch
Mins : Secs
00:00

Fill in the missing digit for each question below.

1) $90 - 2\boxed{} = 67$

2) $90 - 4\boxed{} = 49$

3) $90 - \boxed{}6 = 54$

4) $90 - 1\boxed{} = 72$

5) $90 - 5\boxed{} = 31$

6) $90 - \boxed{}7 = 43$

7) $90 - \boxed{}9 = 11$

8) $90 - \boxed{}3 = 7$

9) $90 - 3\boxed{} = 56$

10) $90 - 8\boxed{} = 8$

11) $90 - 55 = \boxed{}5$

12) $90 - 63 = 2\boxed{}$

13) $90 - 48 = \boxed{}2$

14) $90 - 12 = \boxed{}8$

15) $90 - 79 = \boxed{}1$

16) $90 - 35 = \boxed{}5$

17) $90 - 64 = \boxed{}6$

18) $90 - 59 = 3\boxed{}$

19) $90 - 53 = \boxed{}7$

20) $90 - 21 = \boxed{}9$

Time taken:

$\boxed{}$ minutes and

$\boxed{}$ seconds.

15

Number Lines

Fill in the missing numbers on these number lines.

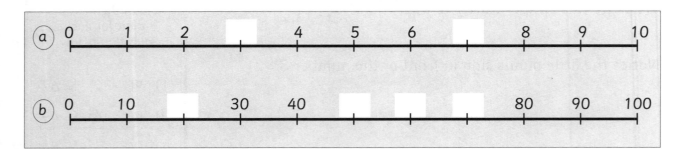

The numbers on this line go up in twos:

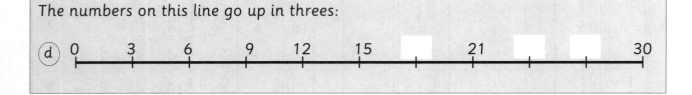

The numbers on this line go up in threes:

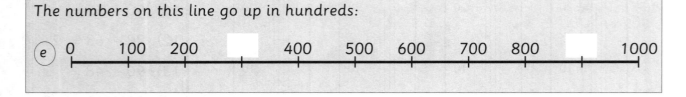

The numbers on this line go up in hundreds:

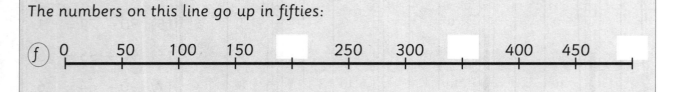

The numbers on this line go up in fifties:

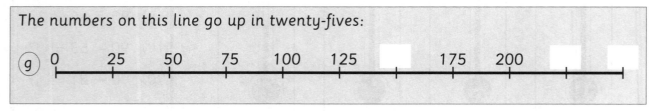

The numbers on this line go up in twenty-fives:

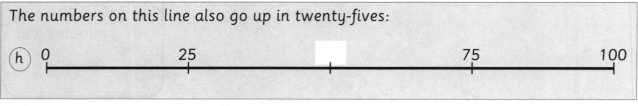

The numbers on this line also go up in twenty-fives:

16

Number lines don't always start at zero.

Look carefully at each number line before filling in the missing numbers.

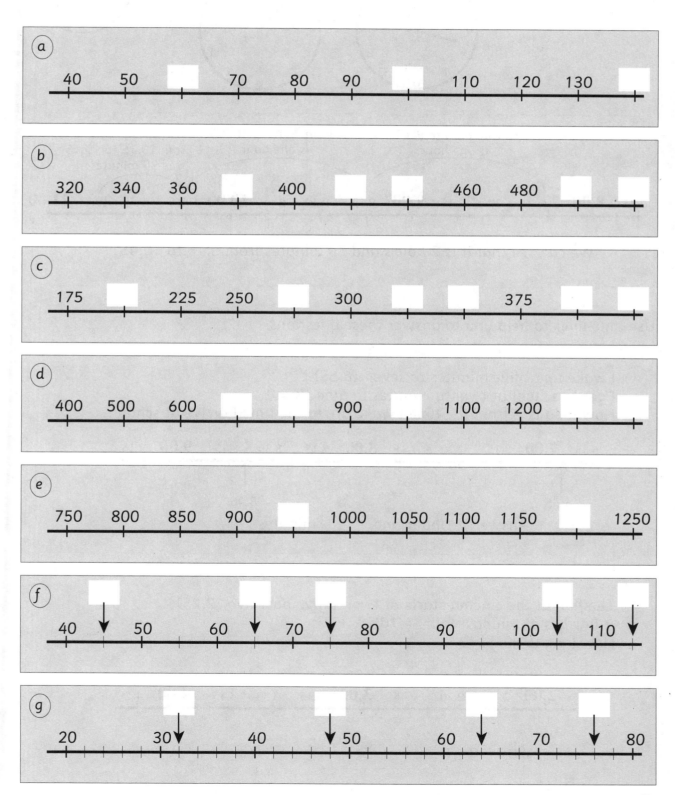

a 40 50 [ ] 70 80 90 [ ] 110 120 130 [ ]

b 320 340 360 [ ] 400 [ ] [ ] 460 480 [ ] [ ]

c 175 [ ] 225 250 [ ] 300 [ ] [ ] 375 [ ] [ ]

d 400 500 600 [ ] [ ] 900 [ ] 1100 1200 [ ] [ ]

e 750 800 850 900 [ ] 1000 1050 1100 1150 [ ] 1250

f [ ] 40 [ ] 50 60 [ ] 70 [ ] 80 90 100 [ ] 110 [ ]

g 20 30 [ ] 40 [ ] 50 60 [ ] 70 [ ] 80

Number Lines, continued ...

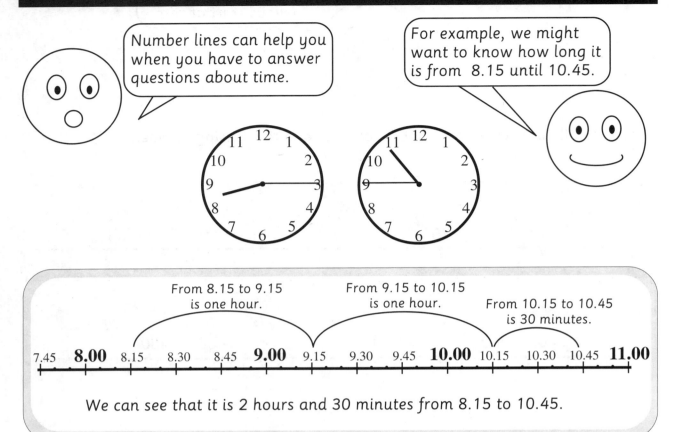

Number lines can help you when you have to answer questions about time.

For example, we might want to know how long it is from 8.15 until 10.45.

From 8.15 to 9.15 is one hour.

From 9.15 to 10.15 is one hour.

From 10.15 to 10.45 is 30 minutes.

7.45 **8.00** 8.15 8.30 8.45 **9.00** 9.15 9.30 9.45 **10.00** 10.15 10.30 10.45 **11.00**

We can see that it is 2 hours and 30 minutes from 8.15 to 10.45.

Use time-lines to help you to answer these questions:

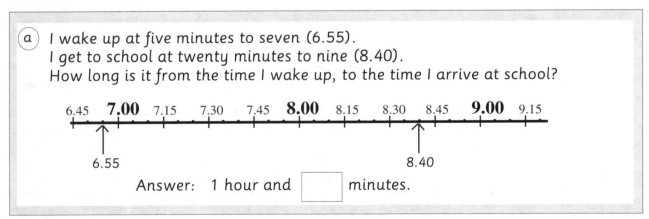

(a) I wake up at five minutes to seven (6.55).
I get to school at twenty minutes to nine (8.40).
How long is it from the time I wake up, to the time I arrive at school?

6.45 **7.00** 7.15 7.30 7.45 **8.00** 8.15 8.30 8.45 **9.00** 9.15

6.55

8.40

Answer: 1 hour and ☐ minutes.

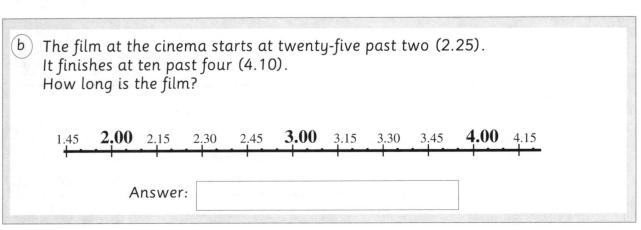

(b) The film at the cinema starts at twenty-five past two (2.25).
It finishes at ten past four (4.10).
How long is the film?

1.45 **2.00** 2.15 2.30 2.45 **3.00** 3.15 3.30 3.45 **4.00** 4.15

Answer: ☐

Number lines can help you to understand fractions and decimals.

The multiplication square on page 20 may help you with these questions:

Number Speed

Digital Stopwatch
Mins : Secs
00:00

This number line starts at zero and finishes at one.

These numbers are called fractions.

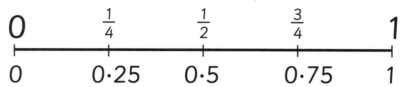

$0 \qquad \frac{1}{4} \qquad \frac{1}{2} \qquad \frac{3}{4} \qquad 1$

$0 \qquad 0{\cdot}25 \qquad 0{\cdot}5 \qquad 0{\cdot}75 \qquad 1$

These numbers are called decimals.

By looking at the number line, you can see that:

a half   is the same as   zero point five

a quarter   is the same as   zero point two five

three quarters   is the same as   zero point seven five.

(a) Write the correct fractions to fill the boxes; the first three have been done for you:

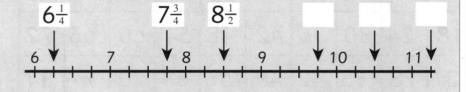

(b) Write the correct decimals to fill the boxes; the first three have been done for you:

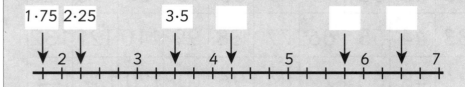

1) $\frac{1}{4}$ of 20 =

2) $\frac{1}{2}$ of 40 =

3) $\frac{1}{4}$ of 12 =

4) $\frac{1}{4}$ of 8 =

5) $\frac{1}{4}$ of 40 =

6) $\frac{1}{4}$ of 24 =

7) $\frac{1}{2}$ of 18 =

8) $\frac{1}{2}$ of 24 =

9) $\frac{1}{4}$ of 32 =

10) $\frac{1}{2}$ of 12 =

11) $\frac{1}{2}$ of 6 =

12) $\frac{1}{4}$ of 28 =

13) $\frac{1}{4}$ of 10 =

14) $\frac{1}{4}$ of 16 =

15) $\frac{1}{2}$ of 7 =

16) $\frac{1}{2}$ of 50 =

17) $\frac{1}{2}$ of 30 =

18) $\frac{3}{4}$ of 8 =

19) $\frac{3}{4}$ of 12 =

20) $\frac{1}{4}$ of 6 =

Time taken:

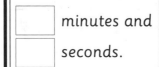

minutes and

seconds.

Multiplication tables

You need to know all of the multiplication tables.

This table square shows all the multiplication tables up to twelve.

If we want to find 5 x 7, for example,
we look along the 5 row and down the 7 column.
Where these cross, we find the answer 35.

You could look along the 7 row and down the 5 column;
the answer would be the same.

x	1	2	3	4	5	6	7	8	9	10	11	12
1	1	2	3	4	5	6	7	8	9	10	11	12
2	2	4	6	8	10	12	14	16	18	20	22	24
3	3	6	9	12	15	18	21	24	27	30	33	36
4	4	8	12	16	20	24	28	32	36	40	44	48
5	5	10	15	20	25	30	35	40	45	50	55	60
6	6	12	18	24	30	36	42	48	54	60	66	72
7	7	14	21	28	35	42	49	56	63	70	77	84
8	8	16	24	32	40	48	56	64	72	80	88	96
9	9	18	27	36	45	54	63	72	81	90	99	108
10	10	20	30	40	50	60	70	80	90	100	110	120
11	11	22	33	44	55	66	77	88	99	110	121	132
12	12	24	36	48	60	72	84	96	108	120	132	144

Page 2
a 388 b 655 c 730 d 741 e 605 f 900
g 493 h 671 i 628 j 325 k 756 l 600

Page 3
a 515 b 892 c 295 d 968 e 736 f 725

Number Speed: 1 20 2 40 3 50 4 60 5 100 6 100 7 20 8 40 9 50 10 60
11 20 12 30 13 40 14 50 15 60 16 70 17 80 18 90 19 100 20 100

Page 5
a 5395 b 9130 c 8816 d 9159 e 5000 f 4557 g 7259
h 5 i 50 j 500

Page 6
a 171 b 421 c 413 d 412 e 361 f 311

Page 7
a 621 b 328 c 424 d 514
e 375 f 581 g 263 h 302 i 126 j 354 k 448 l 582
m 58 n 560 o 411 p 69

Number Speed: 1 4 2 14 3 24 4 34 5 74 6 6 7 26 8 96 9 5 10 15
11 45 12 6 13 16 14 26 15 76 16 5 17 15 18 55 19 8 20 38

Page 8
a 461 b 101 c 721 d 432 e 527 f 192 g 164 h 161
i 479 j 456 k 445 l 330

Page 9
a 4411 b 3634 c 5354 d 3704 e 1597 f 1767 g 2179

Number Speed: 1 3 2 3 3 7 4 7 5 8 6 7 7 12 8 4 9 5 10 6
11 4 12 5 13 6 14 7 15 8 16 9 17 18 18 19 19 13 20 13

Page 10
a 6 b 8 c 10 d 11 e 3 f 15

Page 11

Object	Tally	Number
Aeroplane	ЖНТ ЖНТ ЖНТ ЖНТ ЖНТ ЖНТ |	31
Boat	ЖНТ ЖНТ ЖНТ |||	18

Page 12

Letter	Tally	Number	Letter	Tally	Number
a	ЖНТ ЖНТ ||	12	n	||	4
b	|/	2	o	ЖНТ |||	8
c	|/||	4	p	|||	3
d	ЖНТ |	6	q		0
e	ЖНТ ЖНТ ||ЖНТ|||	19	r	ЖНТ ||||	9
f	||	2	s	ЖНТ |	6
g	||	2	t	ЖНТ ||||	9
h	ЖНТ ЖНТ	10	u	ЖНТ ||	7
i	ЖНТ ||||	9	v	|	1
j		0	w	ЖНТ |	6
k	|	1	x		0
l	ЖНТ |||	8	y	/	1
m	||||	4	z	|	1

Page 13

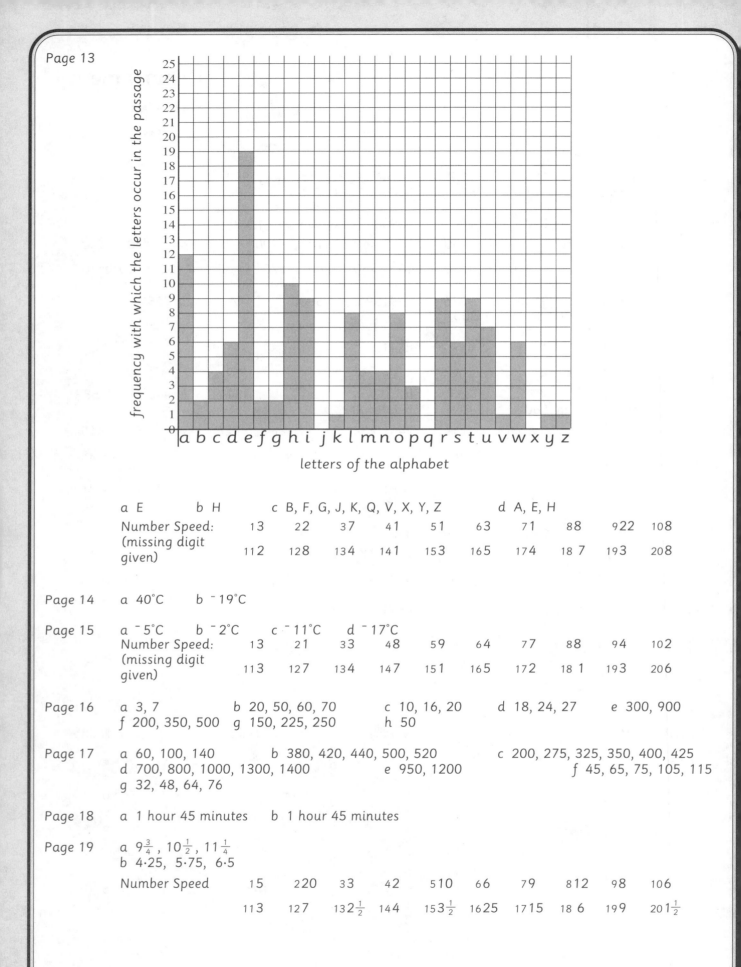

frequency with which the letters occur in the passage

letters of the alphabet

a E   b H   c B, F, G, J, K, Q, V, X, Y, Z   d A, E, H

Number Speed:	13	22	37	41	51	63	71	88	922	108
(missing digit given)	112	128	134	141	153	165	174	187	193	208

Page 14   a 40°C   b ⁻19°C

Page 15   a ⁻5°C   b ⁻2°C   c ⁻11°C   d ⁻17°C

Number Speed:	13	21	33	48	59	64	77	88	94	102
(missing digit given)	113	127	134	147	151	165	172	181	193	206

Page 16   a 3, 7   b 20, 50, 60, 70   c 10, 16, 20   d 18, 24, 27   e 300, 900
ƒ 200, 350, 500   g 150, 225, 250   h 50

Page 17   a 60, 100, 140   b 380, 420, 440, 500, 520   c 200, 275, 325, 350, 400, 425
d 700, 800, 1000, 1300, 1400   e 950, 1200   ƒ 45, 65, 75, 105, 115
g 32, 48, 64, 76

Page 18   a 1 hour 45 minutes   b 1 hour 45 minutes

Page 19   a $9\frac{3}{4}$, $10\frac{1}{2}$, $11\frac{1}{4}$
b 4·25, 5·75, 6·5

Number Speed	15	220	33	42	510	66	79	812	98	106
	113	127	$132\frac{1}{2}$	144	$153\frac{1}{2}$	1625	1715	186	199	$201\frac{1}{2}$

Page 21

x	2	7	5	3
4	8	28	20	12
8	16	56	40	24
2	4	14	10	6
7	14	49	35	21

x	9	11	6	4
3	27	33	18	12
5	45	55	30	20
7	63	77	42	28
4	36	44	24	16

x	9	12	8	3
7	63	84	56	21
5	45	60	40	15
4	36	48	32	12
11	99	132	88	33

x	9	4	6	8
2	18	8	12	16
4	36	16	24	32
6	54	24	36	48
8	72	32	48	64

x	2	3	4	5
2	4	6	8	10
3	6	9	12	15
4	8	12	16	20
5	10	15	20	25

x	6	7	8	9
6	36	42	48	54
7	42	49	56	63
8	48	56	64	72
9	54	63	72	81

Page 22 a 72   b 54   c 92   d 85   e 78   f 98
g 215   h 192   i 273   j 348   k 308   l 768

Page 23 a 1664   b 1422   c 796   d 5247   e 1188   f 2585
g 1728   h 3493   i 7248
Number Speed: 14   26   36   410   58   68   79   86   912   104
115   127   139   148   159   163   175   18 12   197   206

Page 24 a 4   b 6   c 7   d 8   e 9   f 8
g 4 r 2   h 4 r 1   i 5   j 7 r 3   k 9   l 10 r 3

Page 25 a 23   b 32   c 22   d 11   e 32   f 24
g 34   h 21   i 33   j 22   k 12   l 22
Number Speed: 13 r 3   26 r 3   36 r 5   44 r 6   511   69 r 5   72 r 2   89   96   104 r 6
115 r 2   127 r 1   137 r 4   149 r 1   152 r 7   168 r 3   176 r 4   18 1   191 r 8   207

Page 26 a 16   b 48   c 19 r 3   d 17
e 15   f 13 r 2   g 29   h 12 r 1

Page 27 a 226   b 267   c 156   d 189 r 4   e 139 r 3
f 115   g 137 r 2   h 499 r 1   i 153
Number Speed: 12 r 1   25 r 3   39 r 2   44 r 2   53 r 1   67 r 3   76   88 r 4   94 r 4   105 r 2
116   123 r 5   134 r 7   146 r 7   159 r 3   168   174   18 7   1910   205

Page 28 a 80   b 59 r 2   c 166 r 2   d 40

Page 29 a 576   b 84   c 221   d 44   e 89   f 364   g 420   h 16
i 3102

Page 31 a Rhombus   b Rectangle   c Parallelogram   d Square   e Square
f Trapezium

Page 32 a 6·3 cm   b 8·5 cm   c 3·1 cm   d 10·8 cm   e 5·5 cm   f 0·7 cm

Page 33 a approximately 16 cm   b 16 cm   c Rhombus

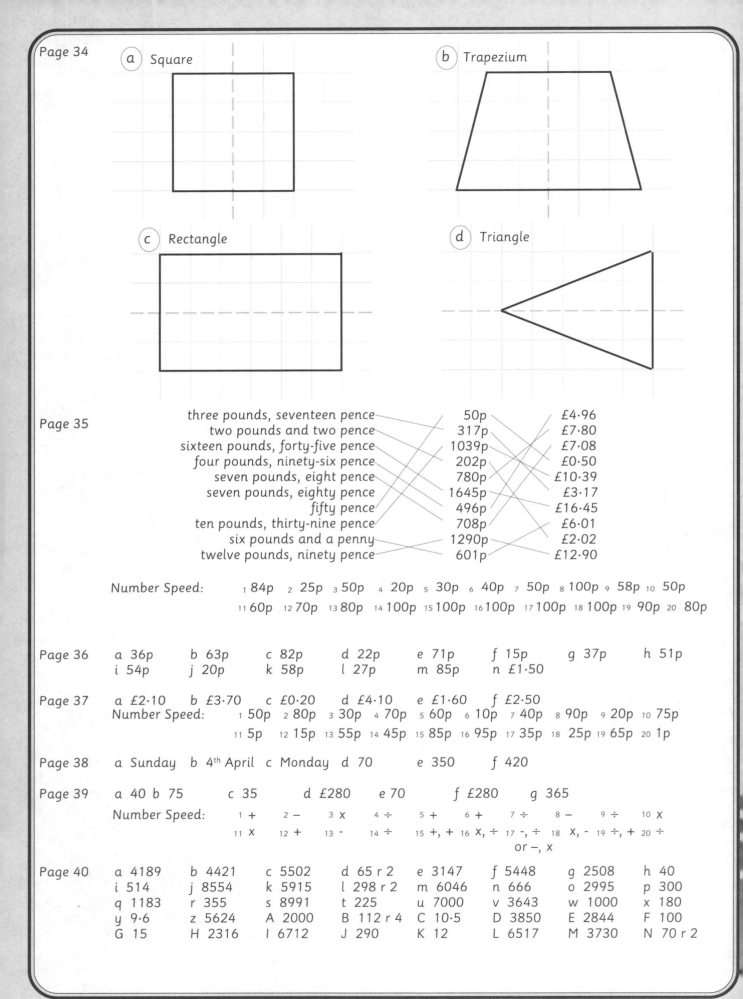

Page 34

(a) Square

(b) Trapezium

(c) Rectangle

(d) Triangle

Page 35

three pounds, seventeen pence
two pounds and two pence
sixteen pounds, forty-five pence
four pounds, ninety-six pence
seven pounds, eight pence
seven pounds, eighty pence
fifty pence
ten pounds, thirty-nine pence
six pounds and a penny
twelve pounds, ninety pence

50p
317p
1039p
202p
780p
1645p
496p
708p
1290p
601p

£4·96
£7·80
£7·08
£0·50
£10·39
£3·17
£16·45
£6·01
£2·02
£12·90

Number Speed: 1 84p 2 25p 3 50p 4 20p 5 30p 6 40p 7 50p 8 100p 9 58p 10 50p
11 60p 12 70p 13 80p 14 100p 15 100p 16 100p 17 100p 18 100p 19 90p 20 80p

Page 36   a 36p   b 63p   c 82p   d 22p   e 71p   f 15p   g 37p   h 51p
i 54p   j 20p   k 58p   l 27p   m 85p   n £1·50

Page 37   a £2·10   b £3·70   c £0·20   d £4·10   e £1·60   f £2·50
Number Speed: 1 50p 2 80p 3 30p 4 70p 5 60p 6 10p 7 40p 8 90p 9 20p 10 75p
11 5p 12 15p 13 55p 14 45p 15 85p 16 95p 17 35p 18 25p 19 65p 20 1p

Page 38   a Sunday b 4th April c Monday d 70   e 350   f 420

Page 39   a 40 b 75   c 35   d £280   e 70   f £280   g 365

Number Speed: 1 +   2 −   3 X   4 ÷   5 +   6 +   7 ÷   8 −   9 ÷   10 X
11 X   12 +   13 -   14 ÷   15 +, +   16 X, ÷   17 -, ÷   18 X, -   19 ÷, +   20 ÷
or −, x

Page 40   a 4189   b 4421   c 5502   d 65 r 2   e 3147   f 5448   g 2508   h 40
i 514   j 8554   k 5915   l 298 r 2   m 6046   n 666   o 2995   p 300
q 1183   r 355   s 8991   t 225   u 7000   v 3643   w 1000   x 180
y 9·6   z 5624   A 2000   B 112 r 4   C 10·5   D 3850   E 2844   F 100
G 15   H 2316   I 6712   J 290   K 12   L 6517   M 3730   N 70 r 2

Removable Answer Section

Number Speed Page

Use your multiplication tables to complete each of these mini-squares as quickly as you can. Some answers are already completed for you.

x	2	7	5	3
4	8			12
8				
2		14		
7				

Time taken to complete:

x	9	11	6	4
3				
5	45		30	
7				28
4				

Time taken to complete:

x	9	12	8	3
7				21
5		60		
4				
11			88	

Time taken to complete:

x	9	4	6	8
2	18			
4				
6			36	
8		32		

Time taken to complete:

x	2	3	4	5
2				
3				
4				
5				

Time taken to complete:

x	6	7	8	9
6				
7				
8				
9				

Time taken to complete:

Multiplication

Complete these multiplications as quickly as you can:

a)
```
    36
x    2
____
```

b)
```
    18
x    3
____
```

c)
```
    23
x    4
____
```

d)
```
    17
x    5
____
```

e)
```
    13
x    6
____
```

f)
```
    14
x    7
____
```

Sometimes we need to multiply quite a big number by some units.

Look what happens when we multiply 36 by 7, for example.

```
    36
x    7
____
```

First, multiply the 6 units by the 7:

6 x 7 = 42

Write the 2 in the units column and put the 4 under the tens.

Now multiply the 3 tens by the 7:

3 x 7 = 21

Add the 4 tens we brought with us:

21 + 4 = 25

Write the 5 in the tens column and put the 2 in the hundreds.

```
    36
x    7
____
     2
 4
```

```
    36
x    7
____
   252
 4
```

Complete these multiplications.
The numbers have already been put into the correct columns for you:

g)
```
    43
x    5
____
```

h)
```
    64
x    3
____
```

i)
```
    39
x    7
____
```

j)
```
    58
x    6
____
```

k)
```
    77
x    4
____
```

l)
```
    96
x    8
____
```

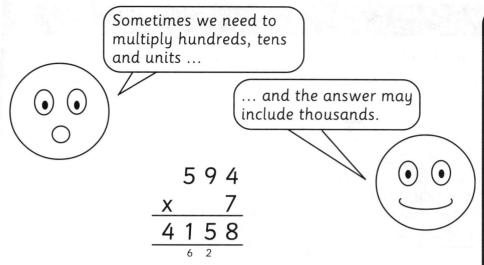

Sometimes we need to multiply hundreds, tens and units ...

... and the answer may include thousands.

$$
\begin{array}{r}
5\ 9\ 4 \\
\times\qquad 7 \\
\hline
4\ 1\ 5\ 8 \\
{\scriptstyle 6\ \ 2}
\end{array}
$$

We start with multiplying the 4 units by 7:

$4 \times 7 = 28$, we write 8 in the units and put 2 under the tens.

$9 \times 7 = 63$, we add the two then write 5 in the tens and put 6 under the hundreds.

$5 \times 7 = 35$, we add the 6 then write 1 in the hundreds and 4 in the thousands.

Try these multiplications.
Remember to write them out correctly.

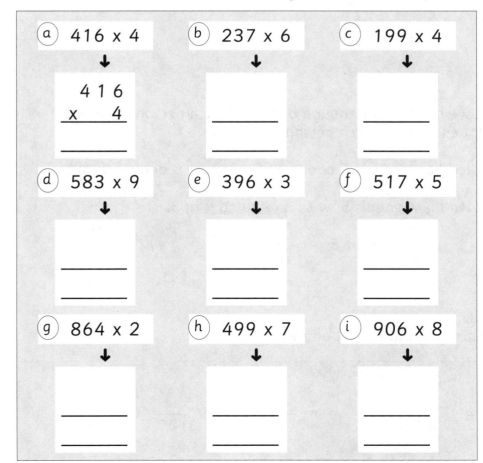

a) 416 x 4
↓

$$
\begin{array}{r}
4\ 1\ 6 \\
\times\qquad 4 \\
\hline

\end{array}
$$

b) 237 x 6
↓
_____

c) 199 x 4
↓
_____

d) 583 x 9
↓
_____

e) 396 x 3
↓
_____

f) 517 x 5
↓
_____

g) 864 x 2
↓
_____

h) 499 x 7
↓
_____

i) 906 x 8
↓
_____

Division

Complete these divisions. They have been written out in two different ways.

(a)	(b)	(c)	(d)	(e)	(f)
36 ÷ 9 =	7)‾4 2	9)‾6 3	48 ÷ 6 =	5)‾4 5	8)‾6 4

The divisions which you have just done have exact answers with no remainders.

Now we will look at some where there are remainders.

For example, suppose we have 23 books to share between 4 people:

23 ÷ 4

We can write the question out in two different ways:

23 ÷ 4 =   or   4)‾2 3

We know that: 20 ÷ 4 = 5

and   24 ÷ 4 = 6 ...

... we can see that we haven't got enough books for each person to have 6, but we have got enough for each person to have 5 ...

... so 23 books divided by 4 equals 5 books, but there are 3 books left over.

We say that 23 divided by 4 equals 5, with a <u>remainder</u> of 3.

23 ÷ 4 = 5 r 3   or   4)‾2 3   (5 r 3)

Complete these divisions.
Some of them have remainders, but not all of them.

(g)	(h)	(i)	(j)	(k)	(l)
34 ÷ 8 =	6)‾2 5	30 ÷ 6 =	7)‾5 2	3)‾2 7	4)‾4 3

Sometimes we cannot find the answer to a division question just by remembering our multiplication tables ...

... But there is a way of working out the answer.

Digital Stopwatch
Mins : Secs
00:00

Some of these divisions have remainders but some do not:

1) $15 \div 4 =$

2) $45 \div 7 =$

3) $59 \div 9 =$

4) $38 \div 8 =$

5) $22 \div 2 =$

6) $59 \div 6 =$

7) $20 \div 9 =$

8) $27 \div 3 =$

9) $36 \div 6 =$

10) $42 \div 9 =$

11) $42 \div 8 =$

12) $29 \div 4 =$

13) $39 \div 5 =$

14) $55 \div 6 =$

15) $23 \div 8 =$

16) $35 \div 4 =$

17) $40 \div 6 =$

18) $7 \div 7 =$

19) $17 \div 9 =$

20) $42 \div 6 =$

Time taken:

◻ minutes and

◻ seconds.

Look at this question:

$$84 \div 2$$

First, write out the question like this: $2\overline{)8\,4}$

Then divide the 8 tens by 2:
$$\frac{4}{2\overline{)8\,4}}$$

Now divide the 4 units by 2:
$$\frac{4\,2}{2\overline{)8\,4}}$$

... and we can see that 84 divided by 2 is 42.

Try these divisions:

a) $3\overline{)6\,9}$

b) $2\overline{)6\,4}$

c) $4\overline{)8\,8}$

d) $5\overline{)5\,5}$

e) $3\overline{)9\,6}$

f) $2\overline{)4\,8}$

g) $2\overline{)6\,8}$

h) $4\overline{)8\,4}$

i) $3\overline{)9\,9}$

j) $3\overline{)6\,6}$

k) $4\overline{)4\,8}$

l) $2\overline{)4\,4}$

More Division

Look carefully at how we divide 74 by 2.

74 ÷ 2

First, divide the 7 tens by 2:	$$\begin{array}{r} 3 \\ 2\overline{)7\,4} \end{array}$$
7 tens divided by 2 gives 3 tens, but there is 1 ten left over. We write this 1 ten next to the 4 units so that we now have 14 units:	$$\begin{array}{r} 3 \\ 2\overline{)7\,^14} \end{array}$$
Now divide the 14 units by 2:	$$\begin{array}{r} 3\;7 \\ 2\overline{)7\,^14} \end{array}$$

... and we can see that 74 divided by 2 is 37.

Here is another example.

78 ÷ 4

First, divide the 7 tens by 4:	$$\begin{array}{r} 1 \\ 4\overline{)7\,8} \end{array}$$
7 tens divided by 4 gives 1 ten, and there are 3 tens left over. We write the 3 next to the 8 units so that we now have 38 units:	$$\begin{array}{r} 1 \\ 4\overline{)7\,^38} \end{array}$$
Now divide the 38 units by 4:	$$\begin{array}{r} 1\;9\;\text{r}2 \\ 4\overline{)7\,^38} \end{array}$$

... 78 divided by 4 is 19, remainder 2.

Complete these divisions.
Write them out in the same way as the ones in the examples.

a) 48 ÷ 3
↓

$$3\overline{)4\,8}$$

b) 96 ÷ 2
↓

c) 79 ÷ 4
↓

d) 85 ÷ 5
↓

e) 90 ÷ 6
↓

f) 93 ÷ 7
↓

g) 58 ÷ 2
↓

h) 37 ÷ 3
↓

On this page we will learn how to divide hundreds, tens and units by units.

Look at this question:

$$379 \div 2$$

First, divide the 3 hundreds by 2.
There is 1 hundred left over which we put with the 7 tens to make 17 tens:

$$\begin{array}{r} 1 \\ 2\overline{)3^179} \end{array}$$

Now divide the 17 tens by 2.
This gives 8 tens and there is 1 ten left over which we put with the 9 units to make 19 units:

$$\begin{array}{r} 1\,8 \\ 2\overline{)3^17^19} \end{array}$$

Divide the 19 units by 2.
This gives 9 units, with 1 left over as the remainder:

$$\begin{array}{r} 1\,8\,9\ r1 \\ 2\overline{)3^17^19} \end{array}$$

… so 379 divided by 2 equals 189, remainder 1.

Complete these divisions:

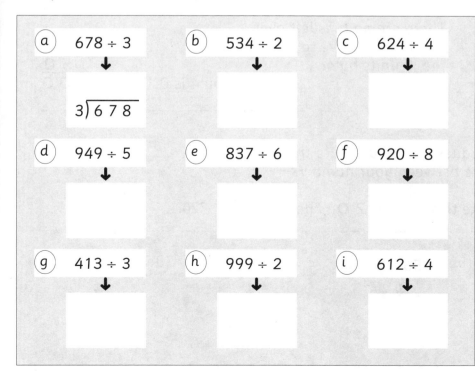

Work as quickly as you can:

1)   15 ÷ 7 =

2)   38 ÷ 7 =

3)   65 ÷ 7 =

4)   30 ÷ 7 =

5)   22 ÷ 7 =

6)   52 ÷ 7 =

7)   42 ÷ 7 =

8)   60 ÷ 7 =

9)   36 ÷ 8 =

10)   42 ÷ 8 =

11)   48 ÷ 8 =

12)   29 ÷ 8 =

13)   39 ÷ 8 =

14)   55 ÷ 8 =

15)   75 ÷ 8 =

16)   64 ÷ 8 =

17)   40 ÷ 10 =

18)   70 ÷ 10 =

19)   100 ÷ 10 =

20)   50 ÷ 10 =

Time taken:

[ ] minutes and

[ ] seconds.

27

Even More Division

Look at how we divide 600 by 8.

$600 \div 8$

First, we try to divide the 6 hundreds by 8:

$$8\overline{)600}$$

... but there are not enough hundreds to be divided <u>so instead we divide 60 tens by 8</u>:

$$8\overline{)600}\ ^{7}$$

60 tens divided by 8 gives 7 tens, and there are 4 tens left over. We write the 4 next to the 0 units so that we now have 40 units:

$$8\overline{)6\,0\,^{4}0}\ ^{7}$$

40 units divided by 8 gives 5 units, with no remainder:

$$8\overline{)6\,0\,^{4}0}\ ^{7\,5}$$

Now look at 600 divided by 4.

$600 \div 4$

First, divide the 6 hundreds by 4:

$$4\overline{)600}\ ^{1}$$

There are 2 hundreds left over. We write the 2 next to the 0 which is in the tens column:

$$4\overline{)6^{2}0\,0}\ ^{1}$$

Divide the 20 tens by 4:

$$4\overline{)6^{2}0\,0}\ ^{1\,5}$$

There are no tens left over ... ... so all we have to do is divide the 0 units by 4:

0 divided by 4 is 0:

$$4\overline{)6^{2}0\,0}\ ^{1\,5\,0}$$

Now try these divisions.
When you write out the questions, make sure that you leave plenty of space between your numbers:

Write them like this: 7 2 0   not like this: 720.

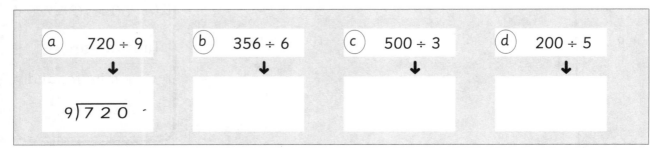

(a) $720 \div 9$	(b) $356 \div 6$	(c) $500 \div 3$	(d) $200 \div 5$
↓	↓	↓	↓
$9\overline{)720}$			

Number Problems

Minnie

Work out the answers to these questions on a separate piece of paper.

You will need to use addition, subtraction, multiplication or division.

Max

a) Some paving slabs are 72 cm long. How many centimetres long is a path which is made of 8 of these slabs?

b) Max and Minnie collect 168 conkers and decide to share them equally between each other. How many conkers will they have each?

c) Minnie has 118 British stamps, 74 French stamps and 29 Irish stamps. How many stamps has Minnie got altogether?

d) How many more British stamps than French stamps has Minnie got?

e) How many more British stamps than Irish stamps has Minnie got?

f) There are 52 weeks in a year. How many weeks are there altogether in 7 years?

g) There are 60 minutes in an hour. How many minutes are there in 7 hours?

h) The tables in the school dining hall can each seat 8 people. How many tables are needed for 128 people?

i) A builder needs 1344 tiles for one roof and 1758 tiles for another. How many tiles does he need altogether?

Lines and Shapes

Lines that run along side each other but never meet each other are called parallel lines.

They are always the same distance apart.

These lines are parallel ...

... and so are these.

This line is horizontal ...

... and this one is vertical.

These two lines meet at a right angle.

These two lines meet, but not at a right angle.

We always show a right angle by drawing a little square in the corner.

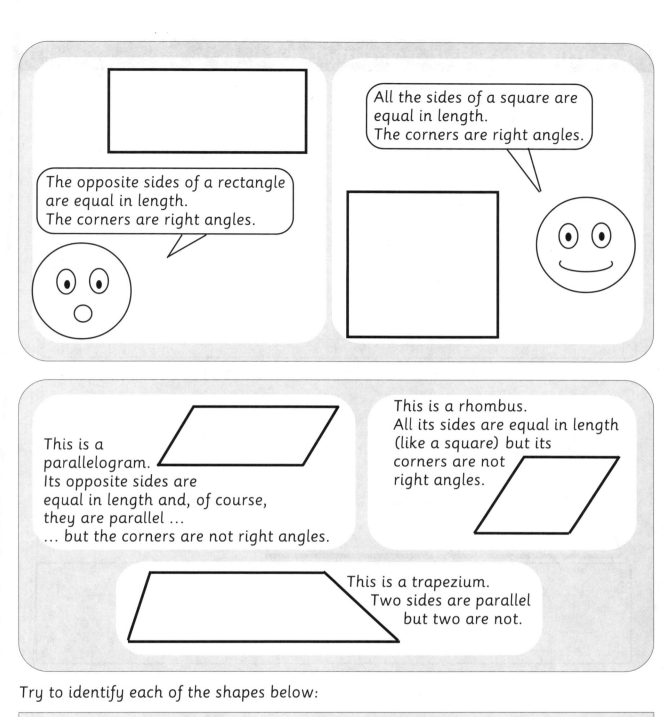

The opposite sides of a rectangle are equal in length.
The corners are right angles.

All the sides of a square are equal in length.
The corners are right angles.

This is a parallelogram.
Its opposite sides are equal in length and, of course, they are parallel ...
... but the corners are not right angles.

This is a rhombus.
All its sides are equal in length (like a square) but its corners are not right angles.

This is a trapezium.
Two sides are parallel but two are not.

Try to identify each of the shapes below:

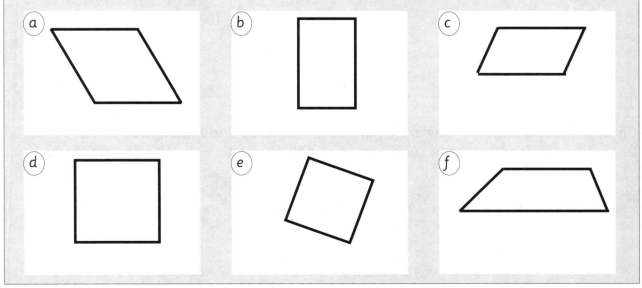

a

b

c

d

e

f

Measuring lines using centimetres

Millimetres are very small. There are ten millimetres in one centimetre.

We say that a millimetre is one-tenth of a centimetre.

This ruler is marked with centimetres and millimetres on this side.

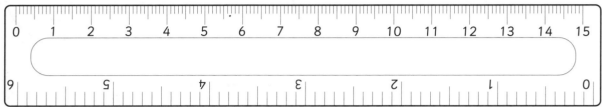

The ruler is marked with inches on this side.

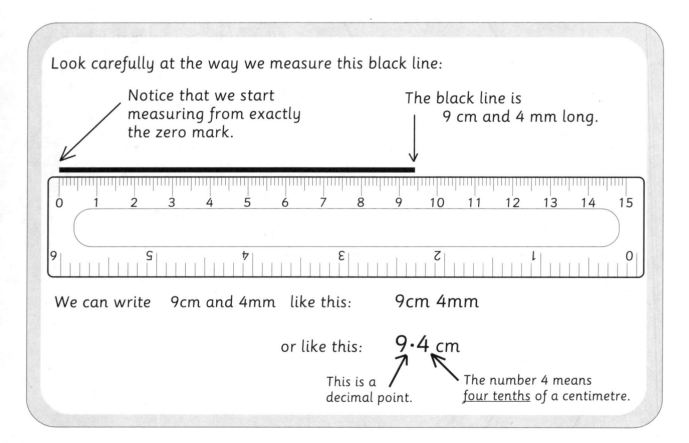

Look carefully at the way we measure this black line:

Notice that we start measuring from exactly the zero mark.

The black line is 9 cm and 4 mm long.

We can write   9cm and 4mm   like this: 9cm 4mm

or like this: 9·4 cm

This is a decimal point.

The number 4 means four tenths of a centimetre.

Change these measurements which are in centimetres and millimetres to centimetres and tenths of centimetres. Don't forget to write the decimal point.

a) 6cm 3mm =   b) 8cm 5mm =   c) 3cm 1mm =

d) 10cm 8mm =   e) 5cm 5mm =   f) 0cm 7mm =

Finding the perimeters of shapes

The distance all around a shape is called its perimeter.

To find the perimeter, we need to measure each side and add the lengths together.

To find the perimeter of this trapezium, add together the lengths of the sides.

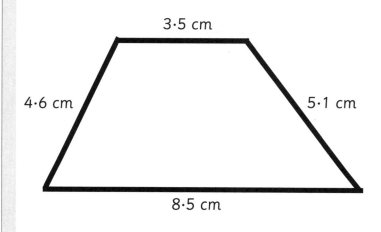

3·5 cm

4·6 cm

5·1 cm

8·5 cm

When you add decimal numbers, make sure that you keep the points in line.

$$\begin{array}{r} 8{\cdot}5 \\ 5{\cdot}1 \\ 4{\cdot}6 \\ + \ 3{\cdot}5 \\ \hline 21{\cdot}7 \end{array}$$

Just add the numbers as normal.

Don't forget to write the decimal point in the answer.

The perimeter of the trapezium is 21·7 cm.

Measure each side then find the perimeter of these shapes:

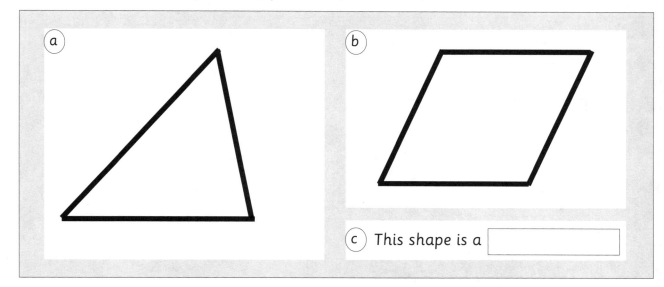

a

b

c) This shape is a ▢

Symmetry

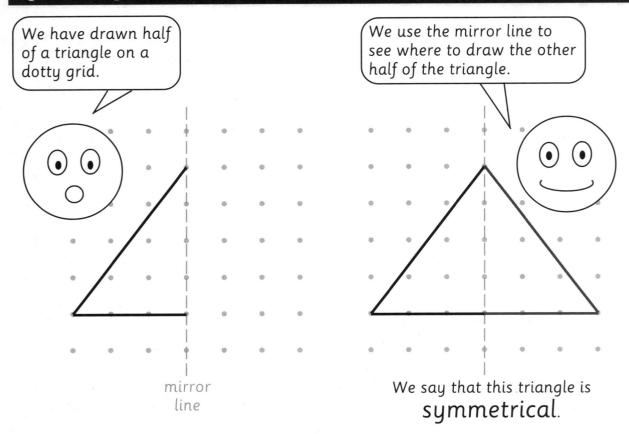

We have drawn half of a triangle on a dotty grid.

We use the mirror line to see where to draw the other half of the triangle.

mirror line

We say that this triangle is **symmetrical**.

Use the mirror lines shown to help you to complete the symmetrical shapes below. Can you name each shape?

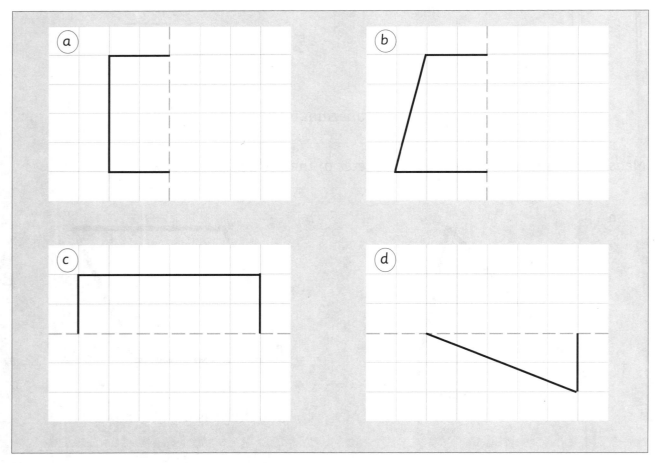

a

b

c

d

In my local shop, a bar of chocolate costs seventy-five pence.

Seventy-five pence can be written in more than one way.

Minnie

Max

Digital
Stopwatch
Mins : Secs
00:00

How quickly can you answer these questions? Time yourself and record your score.

seventy-five pence = 75p = £0·75

Look, there's a decimal point again.

Look at how we write some other prices:

one pound = 100p = £1·00

two pounds, thirty-seven pence = 237p = £2·37

three pence = 3p = £0·03

Join the matching prices. Two sets have been done for you.

three pounds, seventeen pence	50p	£4·96
two pounds and two pence	317p	£7·80
sixteen pounds, forty-five pence	1039p	£7·08
four pounds, ninety-six pence	202p	£0·50
seven pounds, eight pence	780p	£10·39
seven pounds, eighty pence	1645p	£3·17
fifty pence	496p	£16·45
ten pounds, thirty-nine pence	708p	£6·01
six pounds and a penny	1290p	£2·02
twelve pounds, ninety pence	601p	£12·90

1) 63p + 21p =

2) 12p + 13p =

3) 25p + 25p =

4) 11p + 9p =

5) 19p + 11p =

6) 19p + 21p =

7) 29p + 21p =

8) 79p + 21p =

9) 38p + 20p =

10) 42p + 8p =

11) 42p + 18p =

12) 42p + 28p =

13) 42p + 38p =

14) 62p + 38p =

15) 70p + 30p =

16) 71p + 29p =

17) 72p + 28p =

18) 83p + 17p =

19) 43p + 47p =

20) 56p + 24p =

Time taken:

☐ minutes and

☐ seconds.

More Money

If I have a pound and I buy the bar of chocolate for seventy-five pence ...

... you will have twenty-five pence change.

£1 – 75p = 25p

Look at this on a number-line:

| 0p | 10p | 20p | 30p | 40p | 50p | 60p | 70p | 80p | 90p | £1 |

75 pence   25 pence

Here are some more examples:

53 pence   47 pence

81 pence   19 pence

26 pence   74 pence

£1 – 53p = 47p   £1 – 81p = 19p   £1 - 26p =74p

Find the change from one pound when spending these amounts:

(a) 64p ☐   (b) 37p ☐   (c) 18p ☐   (d) 78p ☐

(e) 29p ☐   (f) 85p ☐   (g) 63p ☐   (h) 49p ☐

Now try these:

(i) £2 – £1·46 =   (j) £3 – £2·80 =   (k) £3 – £2·42 =

(l) £2 – £1·73 =   (m) £4 – £3·15 =   (n) £3 – £1·50 =

If I have a five-pound note and I buy two bars of chocolate for seventy-five pence each...

... they will cost one pound, fifty pence and you will have three pounds, fifty pence change.

$$75p + 75p = £1·50$$

$$£5 - £1·50 = £3·50$$

```
0        £1        £2        £3        £4        £5
|||||||||||||||||||||||||||||||||||||||||||||||||
```

| £1·50 | £3·50 |

As you can see,　　£5 − £1·50 = £3·50

　　because　　　£1·50 + £3·50 = £5

Here are some more examples which add up to £5:

| £3·10 | £1·90 |

| £2·70 | £2·30 |

Find the change from five pounds
　　when spending these amounts:

a) £2·90 ☐　　　b) £1·30 ☐　　　c) £4·80 ☐

d) £0·90 ☐　　　e) £3·40 ☐　　　f) £2·50 ☐

Here is another way of finding change from £5:

Suppose I spend　£3·46:

$$
\begin{array}{r}
£5\cdot00 \\
- £3\cdot46 \\
\hline
£1\cdot54
\end{array}
$$

When I spend　£3·46, the change from £5 is £1·54

Number Speed

Digital Stopwatch
Mins : Secs
00:00

How quickly can you answer these questions?
Time yourself and record your score.

1)　£1 − 50p =

2)　£1 − 20p =

3)　£1 − 70p =

4)　£1 − 30p =

5)　£1 − 40p =

6)　£1 − 90p =

7)　£1 − 60p =

8)　£1 − 10p =

9)　£1 − 80p =

10)　£1 − 25p =

11)　£1 − 95p =

12)　£1 − 85p =

13)　£1 − 45p =

14)　£1 − 55p =

15)　£1 − 15p =

16)　£1 − 5p =

17)　£1 − 65p =

18)　£1 − 75p =

19)　£1 − 35p =

20)　£1 − 99p =

Time taken:

☐ minutes and

☐ seconds.

Pictograms

This pictogram shows the number of letters posted in a particular post-box on every day of a week, including Sunday.

You must remember that every picture of a letter represents 10 letters posted.

Pictogram showing letters collected in the South Street post-box, in the week beginning Monday 30th March

= 10 letters

Monday	✉ ✉ ✉ ✉ ✉ ✉ ✉ ✉ ✉ ✉
Tuesday	✉ ✉ ✉ ✉ ✉ ✉ ✉
Wednesday	✉ ✉ ✉ ✉ ✉ ✉
Thursday	✉ ✉ ✉ ✉
Friday	✉ ✉ ✉ ✉ ✉ ✉
Saturday	✉ ✉ ✉ ✉ ✉
Sunday	✉ ✉

Use the information shown on the pictogram to answer these questions:

a) On which day of the week were the fewest letters posted?

b) What was the date when fifty letters were posted?
   Clue: Don't forget that March has 31 days.

c) On which day of the week were the most letters posted?

d) How many letters were posted at the weekend?

e) Altogether, how many letters were posted on week-days? Monday, Tuesday, Wednesday, Thursday and Friday.

f) How many letters were posted in total?

At Nigel's Nurseries, Christmas trees cost £8 each.

Nigel records the number of trees he sells, to the nearest five.

Nigel draws a pictogram to show how many trees he sells in the week before Christmas.

Ten Christmas trees are shown like this:

Five Christmas trees are shown like this:

Digital
Stopwatch
Mins : Secs
00:00

In the questions below the signs + – x or ÷ have been missed out. Write down the missing signs.

1)   7   8 = 15

2) 23   9 = 14

3)   6   5 = 30

4) 24   4 = 6

5) 21 19 = 40

6) 34 12 = 46

7) 60   6 = 10

8) 50 25 = 25

9) 72   8 = 9

10)   7   6 = 42

11) 16   2 = 32

12) 16   6 = 22

13) 16   4 = 12

14) 16   4 = 4

15)   6 2 2 = 10

16)   6 2 3 = 4

17)   6 2 1 = 4

18)   6 2 8 = 4

19)   6 3 2 = 4

20) 100   2 = 50

Time taken:

☐ minutes and

☐ seconds.

Pictogram showing trees sold at Nigel's Nurseries in the week before Christmas

Thursday

Friday

Saturday

Sunday

Monday

Tuesday

On Christmas Eve, the trees are half price.

Christmas Eve

(a) How many trees were sold on Friday?

(b) How many trees were sold on Saturday?

(c) How many trees were sold on Monday?

(d) What is the value of the trees sold on Monday?

(e) How many trees were sold on Christmas Eve?

(f) What is the value of the trees sold on Christmas Eve?

(g) How many trees were sold altogether in the week leading up to Christmas?

39

Mixed Number Practice Page

Practise these additions, subtractions, multiplications and divisions.

Always remember to write your work out neatly. Tidy sums are easier to do.

Write out these questions on a separate piece of paper or in an exercise book.

The first four questions have been written out ...

...so that you can see how they should look:

Addition	Subtraction	Multiplication	Division
264 + 17 + 3908	7418 – 2997	786 x 7	392 ÷ 6

(a)
```
  3 9 0 8
    2 6 4
+     1 7
_____
```

(b)
```
  7 4 1 8
– 2 9 9 7
_____
```

(c)
```
    7 8 6
x       7
_____
```

(d)
```
6) 3 9 2
```

(e) 739 + 2408	(f) 8096 – 2648	(g) 418 x 6	(h) 200 ÷ 5
(i) 126 + 9 + 379	(j) 9453 – 899	(k) 845 x 7	(l) 896 ÷ 3
(m) 3387 + 2659	(n) 900 – 234	(o) 599 x 5	(p) 900 ÷ 3
(q) 211 + 78 + 894	(r) 2000 – 1645	(s) 999 x 9	(t) 900 ÷ 4
(u) 4569 + 2431	(v) 7642 – 3999	(w) 250 x 4	(x) 900 ÷ 5
(y) 6·4 + 3·2	(z) 9111 – 3487	(A) 500 x 4	(B) 900 ÷ 8
(C) 5·6 + 4·9	(D) 6789 – 2939	(E) 948 x 3	(F) 900 ÷ 9
(G) 7·3 + 4·8 + 2·9	(H) 5123 – 2807	(I) 839 x 8	(J) 870 ÷ 3
(K) 6·8 + 5·2	(L) 7495 – 978	(M) 746 x 5	(N) 632 ÷ 9

1. Miss Wood's class had 120 pencils at the start of the year.

12 children use 5 pencils each.

11 children use 4 pencils each.

How many pencils are left at the end of the year?

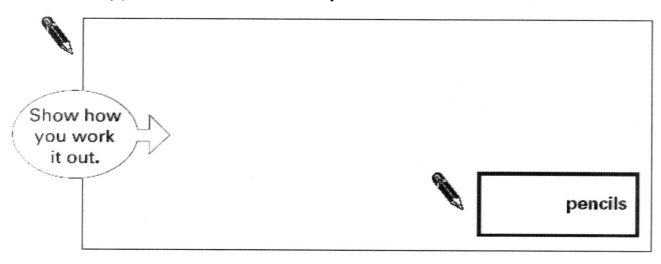

Show how you work it out.

pencils

2.   It costs Ben **£4.16** to post **two** parcels.

One parcel costs **£3.32** to post.

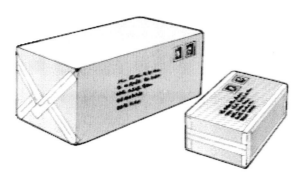

How much does the **other** parcel cost to post?

1 mark

3.   Calculate **438 − 296**

1 mark

4. Here are five number cards.

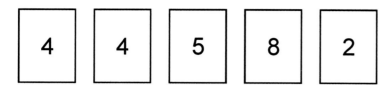

Use all five cards to make an addition that has the **answer 500**

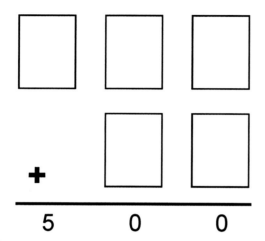

5   0   0

1 mark